House Poor to Real Estate Millions

How I Almost Went Bankrupt Hoarding Houses

© 2023 Grab the Map LLC

Written By Johnoson Crutchfield

GrabTheMap.com

Paperback ISBN: 9798867697709

House Poor *to* REAL ESTATE MILLIONS

How I Almost Went Bankrupt Hoarding Houses

Dr. Johnoson Crutchfield, Jr.

Chapter 1: I Am Writing This While on the Real Estate Roller Coaster Ride

Right now, I'm in the middle of managing cashflow issues. I'm in the middle of banks potentially foreclosing on properties. I'm in the middle of investors needing to be paid back, who lent me money to grow my business, and I'm fighting for my life.

I will not quit. I will not give up. I will do everything I can to make everyone whole, that I promised to make whole. This type of resilience is what you have to have as an entrepreneur, especially in a competitive industry like real estate.

This type of resilience is important to accomplish your dreams. Hold on and you will get through challenging times. I don't know exactly how it will all turn out, but I know it will turn out. When it turns out, I'll have more experience and background. I'll have stronger, deeper relationships because those relationships that survive situations like these, are the ones that survive a lifetime.

I decided to write this book while going through the experiences so that I could tell you how it feels to not know where you will come up with the next payroll check for your team, so I can tell you how it feels.

To have the pressure of banks calling you, asking you for payments, to have the pressure of knowing you want to pay back investors, but not knowing where it will come from. To have the pressure of projects that have failed, to have the pressure of knowing that you took big swings and big action, but that it didn't quite pan out exactly how smooth and easy you thought it would.

BRRRR Investor

Let me introduce myself. I'm Johnoson Crutchfield, and I'm what you call a BRRRR investor. This term became popular in the mid-2000s as a strategy to build equity by adding value to properties that were not fixed up. BRRRR stands for Buy, Renovate, Rent, Refinance, and Repeat.

I like to buy distressed properties that need work, fix them, and rent them out to tenants at a price that would generate long-term cash flow. Then, I go to a bank and refinance the property onto long-term debt, repeating this process.

A great example of this strategy would be my first property purchase. I bought a property for $15,000 in Mississippi, so I know it's a meager price. It was in a very horrible condition with a poor roof. The property needed everything - painting, flooring, roof replacement, new tubs, flaking paint everywhere, and new windows. It was a terrible property.

However, I bought the property for $15,000, and my family and I renovated it ourselves. We bought the materials on a credit card and spent every day fixing up the property after work. Ultimately, we spent about $30,000 to rehab the property, including new windows, a new roof, paint, flooring, bathrooms, and a new kitchen.

Once the property was renovated, I went to the bank, and they appraised it for $85,000. Based on that $85,000, they were willing to lend me about $68,000. However, I only had $45,000 invested in the property adding up my purchase price and the renovations.

I was able to cash out $22,000 on that property, keep it as a long-term rental, and pay back the credit cards and everything I had initially borrowed to finance the project.

This is a powerful example of how the BRRRR strategy can help you build a real estate portfolio. It does require some money upfront, but it allows you to grow a portfolio with unlimited deals because you're recycling the same money over and over.

Throughout this book, I will be sharing lessons on how I used this strategy to create a real estate portfolio worth over $30 million and how I still use this strategy to grow my portfolio. However, there will also be warnings to ensure you do it better and make the most of this strategy. I hope this strategy can help you become even more successful.

"Present" Success Eluded Me

One of the worst feelings when running a business with employees is the possibility of being unable to secure deals to sustain operations. There were weeks when I needed to figure out where payroll would come from— to pay employees and myself. There were weeks when bill collectors called for payments, and we had to defer payments to maintain necessary cash in the bank.

The real issue became evident when I realized I owned hundreds of houses, generating hundreds of thousands of dollars a month in revenue, yet I still struggled to make basic payments. It's hard to imagine that someone with this number of houses would need help paying bills like light, water, and gas bills for properties. These payments should be manageable when building a business the correct way. Nonetheless, even with substantial income, assistance is necessary during such challenging times.

I felt constant anxiety, worry, stress, pressure, and unrest. Despite chasing a dream and future success, present success eluded me.

Real estate is a long-term endeavor. Rental property and the BRRRR strategy (Buy, Rehab, Rent, Refinance, Repeat) are long-term strategies. I should have also considered immediate needs, balancing the short- and long-term.

If I had that goal to seek both immediate cash and the long-term potential of the BRRRR strategy, I would ensure that property rehab was of the highest quality, maximizing property appraisal value and, consequently, the ability to cash out funds. This would allow me to reimburse myself for property purchase and rehab expenses and set aside reserves for future expenses and growth.

I would exercise caution in using the BRRRR strategy for all properties. Some properties accumulate significant equity and demand in the market, making it more advantageous to sell the property and realize gains to supplement income. This approach also helps maintain a steady cash flow.

Discussion Questions

When you started your business, did you think everything would be easy?

What variability did you think there would be in your business?

Key Takeaways

The ups and downs of business are inevitable. Predict these ups and downs as best you can and plan for them.

Claim Your Free Gift

Get your free guide: The Top 10 Mistakes I Made in Real Estate... So You Don't Have To!

GrabTheMap.com/coaching

Chapter 2: Realize Your Addiction Too Late: You Can Be Addicted to Buying Real Estate

You can be addicted to buying real estate. Just like you can be addicted to destructive behaviors, you can be addicted to seemingly progressive behaviors.

Many times, we think about addictions as negative. We think about addictions to negative substances.

Think about the heroin addict, meth addict, cocaine addict, or someone addicted to opioids. We think, why would they do that? Why would they do something so harmful and painful? Why would they hurt their friends and family? Why would they not stop when they could see what drastic and terrible effects would happen because of the last three years of addictive behavior?

9

How to Become House Poor

I've been addicted to buying houses. I'm not comparing this to these drug addictions and the negative consequences they could have, but it is destructive. This is how to become house poor.

I took every bit of cash I would see in my bank account and leveraged it into more houses, more apartments, more warehouses— every time a balance stayed in the account for more than a few weeks. I looked for another deal to buy.

In some ways this has created a drastic empire on paper. If you looked at my personal financial statement, I'm worth millions of dollars— but if you looked at my bank account, you would say, "This guy is broke." You can be addicted to buying real estate. I became addicted to seeing the properties go up in value. I got addicted to seeing the monthly income go up every month.

I became addicted to seeing financial statements showing I was worth millions. I became addicted to buying real estate, addicted to people asking me how many units I had. Addicted to people saying, "You're doing awesome!"

They didn't know my true cashflow situation. When you don't realize you have an addiction, the addiction can have negative consequences.

The addiction can puff up your ego. It can cause you to lose time with your family. It can cause damage to your health, make you not care about your health, and distract you.

The negative effects of addiction, when realized too late, can damage friendships and trusting relationships— people thought they knew you, and then realize you were in trouble.

Based on how I've described the BRRRR strategy to you again (Buying, Renovating, Renting the Property Out, Refinancing, and Repeating), you can visualize how being able to do an unlimited number of deals removes the biggest hurdle that a lot of people face in growing their portfolio.

They often say, "I don't have the money." However, with this strategy, as long as you can find good deals and make good buys, you can buy and hold as many properties as you want.

This brings us to the addiction mentioned in this chapter. Because there is no cap on how much money you can borrow if you're resourceful enough. I would fix up the properties and then go to the bank for refinancing. This period coincided with 2018 to 2023, during which the U.S. experienced some of the lowest interest rates available in modern times. So a lot of the debt was borrowed at three, four, or low 5% interest rates. It seems like a long time ago. In mid-2023, as I write this book, interest rates are at 8, 9, and 10%.

You could easily become addicted to the idea that banks will essentially let you borrow as much money as you want using this strategy. Additionally, you could become addicted to the fact that with this strategy, you can pull out even more money than you put into the property. So, in the example I gave in Chapter One, where I pulled out $22,000 in equity, you could end up putting money in the bank if you execute the strategy correctly.

However, remember that just because the bank will loan you money doesn't mean you should actually borrow the money.

The Truth About Acquiring Properties

When you buy real estate, you're not just acquiring numbers on a spreadsheet— you're purchasing walls, a roof, and everything that comes with it. This includes utility bills, landscaping, and maintenance costs. It also encompasses insurance expenses, property management, and all aspects related to the house. If the roof is old, it becomes your responsibility to replace it. In case of a leak, it falls upon you to rectify it. Any problem associated with the property becomes your issue. This could involve matters like conflicts with neighbors or challenges within the neighborhood.

When we discuss hoarding houses, it's more complex than holding a pack of gum in your pocket. It's more akin to carrying a pack of gum in your pocket without its wrapper. Because outside the wrapper, gum could melt, explode, and cause issues in your pocket.

Similarly, when you have multiple properties, there's a high likelihood that something might go wrong at some point.

An illustrative instance would be when I purchased a duplex, and the neighbor complained about a plumbing backup on their property. The seller from whom I bought the property never disclosed this plumbing issue. However, after buying the property, I encountered problems with the neighbor and had to make repairs to ensure their concerns were addressed. Another property of mine had a tree that posed a risk of falling onto a neighbor's house. A couple of truths emerge when you acquire properties:

1. Often, current tenants or previous owners assume you have ample resources to invest in the property as the new owner. They may inform you about issues that have yet to be disclosed to the previous owner, and you become responsible for addressing those repairs.

2. My attraction to real estate investment originated from growing up with little financial abundance. The realization that buying properties could bolster my income became a driving force. This feeling of having

enough resources to meet my family's needs became addictive. The prospect of always having more money in my bank account than I had spent during the first three decades of my life, and the ability to augment my worth on balance sheets and Excel spreadsheets through this endeavor, fueled my addiction.

3. Addiction often starts when you perceive that your actions are benefiting you. Engaging in property acquisition and hoarding can be advantageous, but it can morph into an unhealthy addiction without considering the concerns outlined in this book.

This addiction prompted me to invest in properties hundreds of miles away, driven by favorable numbers and attractive deals. For instance, despite the considerable distance from Mississippi, I acquired several hotels in a small Iowa town. To navigate this situation, I needed local experience and management. Nevertheless, my craving for favorable deals overshadowed these practicalities. I bought properties in distant locations, assuming they could enhance my revenue and appreciate value.

To avoid succumbing to this addiction, consider this advice:

Seek guidance from individuals who are more experienced than you. Consult those who have managed the number of properties you aspire to own and have scaled businesses to your desired level. Ensure that your end goals align with your entrepreneurial aspirations.

Recognize that this addiction isn't inherently detrimental. Buying and managing properties differs from squandering money on non-assets. This could become a beneficial venture if you address the management issues discussed.

Discussion Questions

Are you suffering from any addictions? How do these addictions affect your actions?

Are there positive things you're addicted to that damage other relationships? How can you manage these addictions?

Key Takeaways

Balance is important to find early in your business. It's hard to balance when you're scaling quickly.

Take time to stop. Pause and assess whether what you're doing is getting you towards your goals. Ask others for help when you feel out of control.

Join Our Coaching Program

Grow your business, meet your real estate goals and achieve success when you join the Grab The Map Mastermind and Coaching Program:

GrabTheMap.com/coaching

Chapter 3: Don't Run Profit and Loss Statements

With the BRRRR strategy in full effect, I could buy houses month after month, right? I would renovate them, rent them out, and refinance them repeatedly. I became so proficient at this process that I established systems to streamline these tasks. There is no limit to the number of real estate holds and transactions you can pursue in a month.

As someone who didn't have much money before starting my real estate business, it was unusual to witness the constant influx of refinance checks into my bank account and the growing monthly rental income I received. Watching the revenue increase was a bit unfamiliar.

I began running the business based on the checking account balance rather than focusing on actual profit and loss statements. I paid attention to how much money was coming in, which I could see was more than before, but I didn't give as much consideration to how much money was going out.

One of the worst things I did in this run-up of houses, is stop tracking profit and loss. In fact, as I bought more properties, I justified negative cash flow months by saying it'll catch up in the end.

I know I'm running at negative $30,000 this month, or negative $10,000 this month. But I'm building up so much equity on paper. My net worth is increasing on paper. I'm paying down debt with the tenant's money on paper, not running profit and loss statements every month, optimizing the cash flow situation so it would be positive cash flow month over month — almost caused me to go bankrupt.

It's important to think about what was going on. I put off today's for potential profit tomorrow. One of the simplest things I could have done in this run up was sell property every now and then, to generate capital.

The strategy I used to build this portfolio is the BRRRR strategy. That's when you buy a property, then you rehab the property. Rent the property out, refinance that property with a bank, and repeat that process over and over again. When you're burning properties as fast as I was, it leaves room for you to see positive cash coming into your account from bank refinances as actual profits in your business.

For a while, those profits will keep you running, make pay your expenses. But when that stops, if you're not positively cash flowing, you will feel it as your cash depletes month after month. Not running profit and loss statements— caring about optimizing your monthly expenses— could bankrupt you.

P&L

Profit and loss statements have become central to the management of my business. They play a vital role in shaping my perspective on the success or failure of my company. These statements indicate whether the business is generating profit or incurring losses. Business owners should have profit and loss statements printed, created, or commissioned every month. Income and Expense Reports provide insight into the business's financial performance, showing whether it's operating at a profit or a loss. Cash flow holds significant importance. In comparison to previous months, a business should strengthen its cash reserves through product sales, asset refinancing, or other forms of private equity funding. Neglecting the measurement of these financial metrics can result in cash flow problems in the future, potentially leading to the financial distress discussed in chapter one— the inability to meet financial obligations, pay employees, and the consequential stress.

Forecasting

Many business owners typically manage their cash by assessing their checking account balance and determining whether they can spend based on its availability. However, this approach is simplistic and amateurish. While it might suffice for day-to-day operations, it fails to provide the capacity to forecast or plan for future periods.

A more effective method to address this issue is by utilizing profit and loss statements. Apart from forecasting income and cash flow, these statements also offer insights into the business's performance, highlighting areas of strength and weakness. They aid in pinpointing expenses that can be reduced and opportunities for revenue generation through adjustments to expenditures.

Analyzing profit and loss statements, I noticed that I was investing significantly in repairs for properties intended for rental purposes rather than properties that could be sold for profit.

This realization prompted a change in strategy. By shifting investments towards properties that were subsequently sold to generate profit, I optimized revenue and enhanced cash flow. This is a specific instance of how profit and loss statements have been instrumental in increasing revenue and cash flow within my business.

Discussion Questions

Do you know how much income your business is making? Do you know how many expenses your business is spending? Are you keeping this track of this somewhere every month?

Are you making excuses for negative cashflow? How long will you make excuses for negative cashflow?

Key Takeaways

Negative cashflow is never okay. Although it may should be immediately addressed to ensure the health of your business. Waiting for cash through the sale of properties or refinances seemed like an eternity, when I needed the money.

I did not take this idea seriously — I was running low on cash until it was too late. Keep a liquidity target. Have a set amount of money in your account to operate your business. It is much more peaceful to know your numbers and track them every month.

Chapter 4: Don't Refinance or Sell to Get Capital Out of Properties

When you realize you're in trouble, the worst thing you can do is delay and procrastinate. Get out of trouble! When you step in quicksand, the best time to get out of that quicksand is when you realize you stepped in it. The longer you wait to get out, the harder it will be to get out.

"Things" happen: damage to your credit report, damage to your reputation, damage to your relationships with vendors, because you stopped sleeping at night. When you've got cash paying on time.

Lenders are less apt to loan you money when it comes across that you need money because of an emergency. be necessary, When your situation is stable and you have control of your finances, it seems to be easier to obtain lender money.

When you need capital, refinance or sell properties right away. It's better to have cash before you need it, than to need cash.

You can access capital from your properties. While I was building my real estate portfolio from 2015 to 2023, interest rates were very low. I sometimes chose not to borrow the equity from a property, leaving some in. This left room for equity in the property when it came time to sell. After fixing up a property and taking it to the bank, they often offered me more money than I had initially invested. This was because they were willing to lend out more money.

Liquidity

Let's say you bought a house for $50,000 and renovated it for $5,000. However, the appraisal might come in at $120,000. Your lender might then offer you a loan for $100,000, allowing you to cash out $45,000 on the property. As you can imagine, this is great cash for many people and would enable them to pursue more deals and have a larger amount of liquid funds.

However, fearing over-leveraging and not wanting to take out all of that money from the property, I often left some of this money within my properties. Sometimes, I chose not to refinance properties after fixing them because I had cash in the checking account. I thought I would leave the equity in the properties to access it if needed.

The problem with this approach arises when you own rental properties and require liquidity for repairs, such as fixing roofs, leaky toilets, and water heaters. As your portfolio grows, you'll also need funds for payroll. The issue with leaving all the equity in the properties is that it reduces your liquidity.

While I was buying properties from 2000 onwards and banks were lending substantial amounts of money, this situation was manageable. However, when I stopped purchasing due to high-interest rates in 2023, this quickly became a problem. Cash flow turned negative due to the expenses on the rentals, and the liquidity or equity needed to improve properties and increase cash flow was tied up in the properties themselves.

The impact on credit reports from making late payments is truly devastating. If you intend to borrow money, you need a credit history that demonstrates a commendable track record. Relationships and reputation contribute to your ability to pay obligations promptly and effectively manage your resources.

You receive more of what you manage skillfully, while your access to what we don't manage diminishes. Take proactive measures to tackle your financial challenges before they escalate into serious issues. What you focus on, grows.

I have since learned the importance of selling or refinancing properties and evaluating each deal individually to avoid encountering this problem again.

Discussion Questions

What are your future capital needs in your business?

How will you make sure you have your capital needs addressed before you need the money? Are there lines of credit or private money lenders you can develop relationships with now, so you have money when you need it?

Key Takeaways

Set a liquidity goal. How much do you need to make sure you can cover expenses and give yourself plenty of time if in a cash crunch?

Refinance or sell before you need the, money so cashflow can be stable and can survive a downturn.

Chapter 5: Don't Hire the Right Team Members

When you plan to grow a business and scale a business quickly, you cannot do it alone.

A big mistake I made early on: thinking I could do everything. When I realized I could not do everything, I began to hire.

When you make the wrong hire, move quickly into the correct hire. Making the wrong hire and sticking with them too long can be costly when you're trying to scale your business quickly.

Not having the roles defined that you need for the next stage of the business is costing you money. It's costing you time, and it's costing you the ability to make your business run efficiently.

Tackling Problems Sooner

I bought two hotels in Iowa that needed a project manager. I did not have a good experience in Iowa — I don't like the extremely cold months.

Hiring the right person on that project would have enabled me to reposition the property sooner, and get cash out. Hiring the wrong people caused costly damages to the property, costly damages to the reputations of the property, and my own reputation as I tried to rebrand the hotels. Hire the right team.

How do you get good at hiring? Get good at firing. You often hire people that are incapable of giving you what you need. When you realize that you hired what you don't need, let it go. It's not about their feelings, it's about what's best for your company.

Not having the right team can be costly. Once, an employee was responsible for collections. She would not consistently contact late tenants behind on their rent. When I asked about this in a meeting, she immediately took action, but when I didn't ask about this in the meetings, the collections were never completed. She would not take responsibility. I left that employee in place for a while. I wanted to be a good boss, but by leaving her in place, with her not doing her job, I was being a horrible boss. Hiring the right team is essential to ensure you don't go bankrupt.

You can do a lot of deals fast and overcome the hurdle of not having any money.

What has become essentially important for me is knowing what I'm good at. And I am good, or rather, skilled at negotiations and finding rental properties. I was so proficient that I often bought five or six deals at a time, not just one. There was even a time when I purchased 30 houses in the same package, all with the plan to buy, renovate, rent, and refinance them. The key here is understanding your strengths and focusing on them.

While I excelled at acquiring houses and rental properties, I recognized the need for a great management team to handle their day-to-day operations. Additionally, I required an efficient administration and back-end office to handle the paperwork involved in refinancing. Skipping this crucial aspect is not advisable. Someone must handle the refinancing process, someone must handle the paperwork, and someone must handle the rental operations. Trying to scale a BRRRR portfolio rapidly while juggling all these responsibilities is nearly impossible. Therefore, adding team members who can assist you swiftly is vital.

But it's not just about adding team members— it's about selecting the right ones to keep projects on schedule and work harmoniously together.

Your Plan and Your Team

Staying ahead of challenges and proactively addressing problems with a well-formed plan and a dedicated team focused on generating more revenue or resolving problematic assets can be highly beneficial. Having a team that excels in problem-solving and tackling issues before they escalate will significantly contribute to your success.

If I could go back and make changes, I would have concentrated on building and training a team that excels in their roles rather than just hiring individuals and leaving them to fend for themselves. Offering coaching and training aligned with their job responsibilities would have been essential.

Hiring individuals with a growth mindset, who believe in their ability to achieve and adapt, and who are willing to tackle challenges by seeking information and expertise would have been a priority.

You need a cohesive team and consistent communication with those members every week. Participate in weekly or daily meetings with your team. Some of our most significant advancements resulted from meetings with our team, enabling collaborative decisions based on the challenges everyone faced. We hold these daily and weekly huddles to ensure our team's progress. Team meetings foster accountability—they establish an understanding that your team expects you to review their work.

Discussion Questions

Do you have the right team members? Do you train team members the right way so they can help you where you need it? Do you hire team members stronger than you, in the areas where you are weak?

Key Takeaways

Hire the right people as soon when you find them, and fire the wrong people. The right team members can make or break you.

Chapter 6: Don't Manage Properties on a Daily Basis

When you don't have the right team, it becomes difficult to manage and keep your eye on multiple projects at the same time. Our properties are managed well, through property managers.

Property managers handle tasks such as collecting rents, collecting outstanding balances, leasing vacant units, and routing maintenance requests from tenants.

When you don't have those employees in place, the properties you want to reposition and add value to will not be repositioned and won't have added value to you. I would buy properties, and they wouldn't be worked on for weeks because I didn't have the right team in place— the right team would've been able to find contractors.

I would have been able to design scopes of work, setup plans for remodel, and monitor those results.

Unfortunately, when you don't manage properties on a daily basis, time flies by quickly. Properties sit, become worse, maintenance only becomes greater, and value goes down.

Mismanaged!

I bought a 44-room hotel with the intention of using the BRRRR strategy. I purchased the property for $380,000 and planned to renovate it for $200,000. The goal was to refinance it for a million dollars once the hotel was stabilized. Since the property was in another state, I hired an employee responsible for overseeing this process. Unfortunately, that employee deceived me about the progress of the work being done for about six months.

When I finally visited the property to assess the progress, I realized it had been mismanaged and not properly maintained. The desired results were not achieved because the necessary actions were not taken. If the property isn't stabilized or generating the expected rental income, you can't proceed with the refinancing. As a result, the money spent on renovating the property remains tied up inside it.

Therefore, it's crucial in chapter six to emphasize the importance of monitoring and managing properties throughout the process.

Another aspect to consider is conducting weekly meetings with your property managers. These meetings facilitate discussions about specific issues they may face and find effective solutions to address project-related challenges and fulfill the property manager's specific needs.

Almost Go Bankrupt

You want to almost go bankrupt. You buy so many houses that you can't keep your attention on them. When I first bought properties, and was doing everything myself, I would make sure contractors were in place the day I closed on the property. Materials were already on site. There was a scope of work ready to execute from day one. By the time I started buying seven, ten, thirty properties at once, those responsibilities were up to different team members. I released those responsibilities so I could focus on buying— but if those responsibilities were not getting handled, I would pay for it.

Neglect happens when you take your eyes off something important. Focus is when you put your eyes back on it.

Focus on your deals, focus on improvement, focus on making money. Focus on excellent management.

Systems and Processes

You will receive more of what you manage and less of what you neglect. When working hundreds of rental properties, you need systems and processes to handle the volume. These systems include paying utility bills, maintaining updated financial records, and comprehensive accounting. You'll need systems for tenant management, rent collection, and handling maintenance orders and requests. The vigilant monitoring and oversight required for these processes can generate substantial profits and create a positive experience for residents and properties. Conversely, such monitoring and oversight can yield positive consequences.

In our case, we employ building and property management software to maintain records of various properties. This enables us to track tenant payment timelines, address maintenance concerns, and keep tabs on unit vacancies through screenshots on a computer screen. However, I'm aware that some landlords do not use such software, relying on Excel spreadsheets and other manual methods for payment management. There are more efficient ways to manage properties.

Furthermore, we have consistently conducted weekly meetings with our property management team for over five years. During these meetings, lasting about an hour to an hour and a half, we share information about maintenance orders, vacancies, outstanding balances, and any pertinent issues impacting our business. These meetings serve as training sessions where we educate each other on relevant matters.

Discussion Questions

Do you have KPIs for managing your properties? Does someone manage your properties every day?

What are you doing for the mismanaged properties in your portfolio? Who can help manage your properties to make sure you make progress every day?

Key Takeaways

What you don't manage will get out of control. What you let sit will deteriorate further.

Stay on top of your "stuff!"

Join Our Coaching Program

Grow your business, meet your real estate goals and achieve success when you join the Grab The Map Mastermind and Coaching Program:

GrabTheMap.com/coaching

Chapter 7: Buying Properties in Multiple Markets with No Boots on the Ground

I was seeing such growth in cash flow, unit count, and recognition for being a great businessman, that my ego got in the way. I thought everything I bought would turn to gold. I started thinking that every project would make money. I started buying properties in locations that I had no business buying.

I was never afraid of buying ugly distressed properties. That was my business. However, when you buy in locations with no infrastructure, no boots on the ground, and no one who knows the area— you take a humongous risk. I did not mitigate for this risk, and it cost me dearly.

One property I bought was in the middle of nowhere, in a town with less than 1000 people. I celebrated the buy because the property was so cheap. Just because a property is cheap does not mean it is a good deal. Consider the location, access to funding, and access to contract labor.

When you buy in remote locations where you have no support, it can be difficult to stabilize properties. Consider this if you want to buy a property 500 miles away from where you live, 50 miles away from the nearest population area.

These small locations often have deals that seem like deals by the numbers, but could be difficult to get your money out of, in the end. Consider how to get boots on the ground when buying in a remote location.

Check your ego to ensure that you make deals for the right reasons. Do you have boots on the ground in the area that can help you manage. and see factors that you can't find on Google Maps.

Find Properties Where the Numbers Work

With the BRRRR strategy, you can pursue deals anywhere as long as you find properties where the numbers work. Some individuals may struggle to find properties that meet their criteria within their local market.

What do I mean by "the numbers work?" In the context of the BRRRR strategy, the total investment, including the purchase price and repairs, should be less than 70% or 75% of the property's loan-to-value ratio. Most banks, when refinancing, will typically lend up to a maximum of 65%, 75%, or 80% if it's a reputable local bank.

Ensure that your project doesn't exceed the loan-to-value limits set by the bank, which would hinder your ability to refinance and extract capital. When introducing the BRRRR strategy, it's important to convey that the numbers need to make sense. Suppose the numbers don't work in your current market due to high competition or inflated prices in major metropolitan areas. In that case, exploring other locations where the numbers align better may be necessary. Traditionally, the Midwest and rural areas in the South have been known to offer more favorable numbers. These are also considered secondary markets.

I am oversimplifying the strategy in this chapter. Still, I want to emphasize that although the BRRRR strategy appears simple, it requires several components to fall into place for success.

Firstly, when you purchase a property, you must ensure the numbers work, which requires thorough underwriting and analysis. This involves someone reviewing the deal, assessing the numbers, and confirming the project is viable. It's a crucial step that requires a person or a well-defined process.

Secondly, the renovations must be completed. This means that someone needs to be involved in the process of fixing up the property, procuring materials, and overseeing the renovation.

Build Relationships

Building relationships with other investors has evolved significantly. Social media has provided an excellent opportunity for testing and networking. Connecting with fellow investors has become easier. I've discovered valuable online communities, paid and free, where individuals are eager to connect, share their experiences, and discuss real estate ventures. Through these communities, it's possible to make global friendships with like-minded individuals with similar goals.

Explore online communities such as the one I oversee, the Grab the Map Community at Facebook.com/GrapTheMap. We have a free Facebook group named the **Wealth in Real Estate** Facebook group and a paid one called the **Grab the Map Mastermind.** These platforms allow people to connect, exchange stories, and establish meaningful relationships with others actively making strides in the industry. Engaging in these groups can lead to valuable connections that prove beneficial.

One of the most significant lessons I've learned in my current business experience is that initial approaches to getting started may be more aggressive, akin to a shotgun approach, where you try various strategies to see what works. The key to success lies in refining your methods based on changing circumstances, emerging insights about yourself and your team, and the effectiveness of your actions.

Progressing in business is best achieved by being a reflective leader who adapts and makes changes based on data and outcomes. This book aims to present a method that can genuinely assist individuals in building substantial wealth and a portfolio without facing capital depletion and underscore the responsibility and accountability of utilizing this method.

Key Takeaways

Have a plan. Who will manage your assets when you manage multiple markets out of your local area?

This is also a good idea when you have property in your local area.

Chapter 8: Borrow a Bunch of Money, Don't Care About the Interest Rates

If you buy several properties quickly, it will take capital. The capital sources you have will be limited when you first start. I bought my first properties using seller financing and credit cards— but consider how you will get money for your first few real estate deals.

Borrowing money from credit cards and from the sellers allowed me to build a multimillion dollar real estate portfolio from scratch. It's a great way to get started in real estate investing, but as I scaled from 1 to 100 to 300 to 500+ units, I continued to borrow money and continued to need more money.

When you borrow this money and you're scaling fast, you probably don't care what the money source it. where it comes from because You think your deal will the interest rates. When you borrow money at expensive interest rates, it gets expensive quickly when those projects do not stay on timeline, or those projects do not execute the way you expected.

One, time I offered to someone 6% per month on his money on a deal. Every month for a year, I deposited 6% per month into his bank account. The project took me longer than expected. His payment almost caused me to go bankrupt.

When you buy several properties fast and you scaling your business, stay well-capitalized. Have access to money. Look at how much that money costs you. You might not be able to get 2% or 3% interest rates, but if your interest rates that allow you to cash flow, that is better than paying interest rates that you cannot escape.

Another time, I borrowed money from a merchant cash advance lender online. He started taking daily deposits out of my bank account. It is so lone-sharky. Don't do it.

Stay organized. Track your lender names, how much you owe them, the interest rate is on your money, and the terms of payback. That can help you as you try to maintain capital in your business.

Using credit cards for debt and growing a real estate business is a popular strategy. This is can be helpful if you get a credit card at 0% for 12-18 months. However, keep in mind that the interest rates on credit cards often go up to 25-40% when you don't pay them off every statement. When you're floating houses on credit cards at 30%, it is impossible to cashflow. Do your due diligence. Ensure you keep track of the interest you're paying. Get out of high interest as soon as possible.

While it might seem appealing to purchase a house using credit cards during the initial year of your business, this approach becomes problematic as you scale. Relying on such a strategy becomes increasingly unfavorable over time. Your CPA will disapprove of your 25-credit card approach when conducting business in this manner. Recognize the advantages of low-interest rates. Acquire knowledge about interest rates and comprehend the cost of borrowing money. Learn as much as possible about the expenses associated with borrowing.

Discussion Questions

Do you know the interest rates, interest rates on all your debts? Do you know which interest rates are high interest and which interest rates are low interest? Do you track your numbers every month?

Key Takeaways

All money should not be borrowed just because they will lend it to you.

Know the terms of the money and the interest rates of the money, and that they fit within the numbers of your deals.

Chapter 9: Don't Communicate with Private Lenders/Bankers

When I realized I was in trouble, my biggest mistake was avoiding the lenders I was paying late. Lenders would call to ask what was going on— I would ignore their calls. I planned to call back, but the feeling in the pit of my stomach of telling them bad news, caused me to avoid them and never call back.

I often looked at their emails, but could never bring myself to respond. At the time, I thought I was buying time, but I was worrying the heck out of my lenders, and ruining their trust about me paying them back.

When I finally spoke to these lenders, they understood that payment was taking longer than expected. They wanted communication.

Communicate with your lenders as soon as possible when your plans go awry.

Also, my attitude was a problem. I became embarrassed. You may think you avoid embarrassment by avoiding your lenders, but you're really making the situation worse.

One of my banks became so frustrated by my delay that they began foreclosure proceedings, and ran my name in the newspaper. This was the worst thing that I could have imagined. Luckily, I stopped the foreclosure, but I could have avoided that damage to my reputation if I picked up the phone or responded to an email.

Maintain Communication

You must maintain communication with your bankers and lenders, particularly when facing cash shortages or financial difficulties. They are accustomed to some projects proceeding as planned and others encountering challenges.

Maintain an open line of communication regardless of the circumstances. Whether projects have experienced delays or deviations from the original plan, engage in discussions with your lenders. Most investors would understand these situations. Regular communication with your lenders is beneficial, regardless of whether the news is positive or negative.

One challenge I faced in the past was being reluctant to deliver unfavorable news. I wasn't comfortable contacting investors to explain the project was not proceeding as anticipated. I did not relish discussing deviations from the plan.

However, communication is imperative. As an investor, you are rewarded for your efforts. You earn your share because you are willing to communicate openly. Your willingness to tackle difficult conversations is why investors you can achieve significant gains. The outcome might be more favorable than anticipated when confronted with difficult discussions.

Some of the most challenging conversations occurred not because a deal went bad or not as planned, but because I was slow about communicating with my investor or even worse, slow to take action on a project to correct whatever the issue was.

Discussion Questions

Are you hiding from your lenders?

Do you find it difficult to have conversations that you don't, that you don't, um, where the news is not good for the lender practice having difficult conversations

Key Takeaways

Practice difficult conversations in the mirror, or with people you trust, then have the conversation with the party that needs the information.

Don't hide bad news— it only gets worse when you don't communicate.

Join Our Coaching Program

Grow your business, meet your real estate goals and achieve success when you join the Grab The Map Mastermind and Coaching Program:

GrabTheMap.com/coaching

Chapter 10: Ruin Your Credit

Another way to go bankrupt: losing the ability to borrow money due to a low credit score. A low credit score is so low means the banks lose confidence that you will repay your loans.

I have never missed a payment, but I noticed my credit score suffered when I maxed out credit cards. Utilization is one of the highest factors that impacts your credit score, and it can result in your credit score dropping hundreds of points because you're maxed out on credit. When you borrow money, keep your credit in good shape. As a real estate investor, people pull your credit to see if you are a good bet, and if you will pay back.

I was once offered an interest rate 4% higher than what I would have been offered if I had perfect credit. Your credit score can be one of the most significant factors that determine whether you can get out of a financial bind.

If you get in a bind and you have a great credit score, you can often borrow, to bridge the gap and get financial help. Buy time to liquidate a property or refinance, then yourself in a better cash position. Keep a good eye on your credit when you run a business, and especially even more when you get in a bind.

I acquired most of my property from sellers who had challenges selling their properties. These sellers were distressed, owning properties in need of extensive renovations. It was often a period in their business when they required immediate cash. I formulated offers tailored to securing the best price and assisting them in their predicament. This approach aligns with one of my core values, which prioritizes integrity over monetary gain. It reflects my belief that ethical considerations need not be compromised for financial success.

With the need to act fast for deals like this, credit can be instrumental in making things happen in time to solve the seller's problem. Good credit also builds additional confidence when you are presenting offers to sellers. If you know you've got that money, that'll make you much more confident in doing the deal.

I've seen person after person ruin their credit by buying things they can't afford, and doing deals they just shouldn't do, and I'd to see one person who reads this book not to realize the tremendous value of their credit.

Discussion Questions

Do you know your credit score and why it is that number?

Are you doing everything you can to protect, protect, or improve your credit?

Key Takeaways

Know your credit score. Protect your credit score at all costs.

Pay your bills on time. Call lenders in advance of any trouble and find out what their credit reporting policies are.

Chapter 11: Throw Ethics out of the Window, Get Deals Done No Matter What the Cost

When you find yourself in a tight spot, the allure of resorting to unethical actions or making poor choices can become intense due to a perceived lack of alternatives. Some people abandon ethical principles when they feel pressure. **I challenge you to uphold your ethics even more fervently during challenges and trials and to steadfastly adhere to your principles in tough times.**

There will always be more deals. It is not worth ruining your reputation or being dishonest to buy properties and grow your company.

Think about deals before relationships. Early on, I lost one of my best friends trying to grow the business. I wanted to make a deal instead of valuing the relationship. Today, I would rather not own that deal and keep the relationship with that investor.

When you scale quickly, you grow, and have great ambition, you realize that life is not only about money. It's also about the journey and the relationships you have along the way. Getting deals done, no matter the cost, may be the most costliest thing you ever discover.

Don't have people sign fake documents. Don't be fraudulent with banks. Don't misuse insurance proceeds. Don't look over your shoulder because you committed an act that could land you in jail.

Temptation gets real when you get in a bind. Keep your morals and to keep your wits in business.

Maintain a good credit score, especially if you intend to borrow money. As an investor, you should be familiar with your credit score and work towards improving it. Develop and protect your credit when acquiring properties. My credit played a significant role in enabling me to refinance, generate cash reserves, and secure loans for my company's needs. If

I had maintained better credit, my journey would have been easier. I would have even more opportunities.

Discussion Questions

Are your ethics temporary or permanent?

Do you surround yourself with people whose ethics are permanent?

Is money or "the deal" more important to you?

Key Takeaways

Your ethics are the most important thing that you have as a person on planet Earth. Keep your word. Integrity is worth more than any deal.

Relationships matter and business is personal, so make your business capable of being personal.

Chapter 12: Your Real Estate Journey is Worth It

Consider how much knowledge and experience that comes from the journey of growing your real estate company. The friends you make, the problems you solve, the adaptability you learn, all makes the journey worth it.

When you look at business building like it's a journey, you stop looking at each stage of business like it's your worse nightmare. The good, the bad, and the ugly are really just a tiny bit of the overall process.

Some of my best learning has come from my biggest mistakes or challenging times in business. Without these times, I wouldn't have made changes to business models, strategies, or built a better business.

I learned about out state real estate investing when my family decided to do more deals in Texas and to come up with ways to manage projects when I was present.

I learned how to use virtual assistants when I continued to face the challenge of finding focused in person staff to help with acquisitions and marketing tactics in-office.

I learned about bankruptcy when I almost went into bankruptcy after buying hundreds of rental properties within just a few years.. Before that, I knew nothing about it. The conversations with bankruptcy attorneys make me a better and more knowledgeable real estate investor. The conversations with my lenders to reorganize payments make me a better borrower when I look at deals.

Knowing more about the process is not a bad thing— and when you get in a bind and use that information, you learn the most. You learn how you and your team handle pressure. You see those unexpected results and you figure out how to adapt. You make strategic plans to avoid those situations in the future.

If you asked me if I would do this journey all over again, the answer is a 100% yes. The lessons I learned were worth the trouble.

Discussion Questions

Are you willing to do hard things? Are you willing to go through the tough seasons?

Are you able to get over mistakes? How quickly can you learn the lesson and get back to work?

Key Takeaways

The journey is worth it. If I can help you in your journey. Reach out to me about the Grab The Map Inner Circle and Mastermind Group. We hold meetings every week, helping people grow their businesses.

If I can help you grow your business, go to GrabTheMap.com and click the coaching tab so that we can help you grow your business.

About Dr. Johnoson Crutchfield, Jr.

Dr. Johnoson (John) Crutchfield is a God-fearing, family-focused entrepreneur and teacher who professionally coaches and mentors other teachers and entrepreneurs in the areas of educational leadership, business, real estate, and faith. John owns a consulting business, as well as a real estate business which acquires and manages single family and multifamily properties, in addition to helping other investors find projects to invest in.

With more than 300 rental units and assets valued at over $20,000,000 in Mississippi, Texas, and Louisiana, John has built relationships with contractors, real estate professionals, and experienced property management companies to develop systems to accurately record rent payments, collect accounts receivable, provide property maintenance to drive and support future growth.

-Formally an Experienced School Principal with a demonstrated history of working in the education management industry. Skilled in Coaching, Classroom Management, Lesson Planning, Educational Technology, and Instructional Design. Strong education professional with a Doctor of Education (Ed.D.) focused in Curriculum and Instruction from University of Louisiana Monroe.

About Grab the Map

Grab the Map is comprehensive real estate investment, property management, and education company committed to helping you and your family find the perfect rental property or investment. We offer single-family homes, duplexes, warehouses, triplexes, and small apartment buildings. Our properties are regularly maintained, inside and out, in order to uphold the quality that makes us great. We take pride in helping our clients find clean, affordable, safe housing, without denying them due to their credit scores.

We also love helping investors get great returns on their capital. We provide opportunities for investors that provide double digit returns.

We also provide business and real estate education, coaching, and consulting services for aspiring and real estate businesses looking to grow their companies.

We specialize in Acquisitions, Rental Property Management, Flips, Educaton, and Investments.

75

www.ingramcontent.com/pod-product-compliance
Lightning Source LLC
Chambersburg PA
CBHW072340290526
45794CB00002B/958